LOGANSPORT CASS COUNTY PUBLIC LIBRARY

ODA, HIDETOM
ANIMALS OF T   T5-COA-324
(3) 1986 J 591.9 ODA S:432270
1501 03 347130 01 4 (IC=0)

Animals of
the Seashore

This book has been reviewed
for accuracy by
David Skryja
Associate Professor of Biology
University of Wisconsin Center—Waukesha.

Library of Congress Cataloging in Publication Data

Oda, Hidetomo.
    Animals of the seashore.

  (Nature close-ups)
    Translation of: Iso no seibutsu / text by Hidetomo Oda, photographs by Hidekazu Kubo.
    Summary: Discusses the life cycle and behavior patterns of crabs, sea anemones, sea snails, and other creatures of the seashore.
    1. Seashore biology—Juvenile literature. [1. Seashore biology] I. Kubo, Hidekazu, ill. II. Title.
III. Series.
QH95.7.03513   1986   591.909′46   85-28192
ISBN 0-8172-2543-9 (lib. bdg.)
ISBN 0-8172-2568-4 (softcover)

This edition first published in 1986 by Raintree Publishers Inc.

Text copyright © 1986 by Raintree Publishers Inc., translated by Jun Amano from *Creatures of the Seashore* copyright © 1978 by Jun Nanao and Hidetomo Oda.

Photographs copyright © 1978 by Hidekazu Kubo.

World English translation rights for *Color Photo Books on Nature* arranged with Kaisei-Sha through Japan Foreign-Rights Center.

All rights reserved. No part of this book may be reproduced or utilized in any form or by any means, electronic or mechanical, including photocopying, recording, or by any information storage and retrieval system, without permission in writing from the Publisher. Inquiries should be addressed to Raintree Publishers Inc., 310 W. Wisconsin Avenue, Milwaukee, Wisconsin 53203.

2 3 4 5 6 7 8 9 0   90 89 88 87

Animals of the Seashore

Raintree Publishers
Milwaukee

◀ **A rocky seashore.**

There are various kinds of seashores: sandy, muddy, or rocky. Each type has its own variety of sea creatures.

▶ **These shells are the homes of seashore animals.**

The tiny cone-shaped shells are cemented to the rocks by barnacles. The larger shells in the middle are made by limpets, which rub their shells into the rock's surface to anchor them.

Thousands of tiny animals live in the depths of the ocean, on sandy beaches, and along rocky shorelines. Snails, clams, oysters, crabs, sea anemones, and a host of other creatures have adapted, over the centuries, to a life bordering on land and sea. The shoreline changes daily with the ebb and flow of the ocean's tide. Some seashore animals spend their entire lives underwater. Others are born in the ocean, spend their adult lives on shore, and then return to the ocean to lay their eggs.

Although the seashore is teeming with life, most of it is invisible when the ocean tide is high. But when the tide goes out twice a day, it leaves behind a fascinating variety of clam shells, starfish, sea urchins, snails, and scuttling crabs.

▶ **A shore crab peeping out from beneath a rock.**

Even when the tide goes out, it is not always easy to find sea creatures. This shore crab is well camouflaged because its color blends with the rock under which it hides.

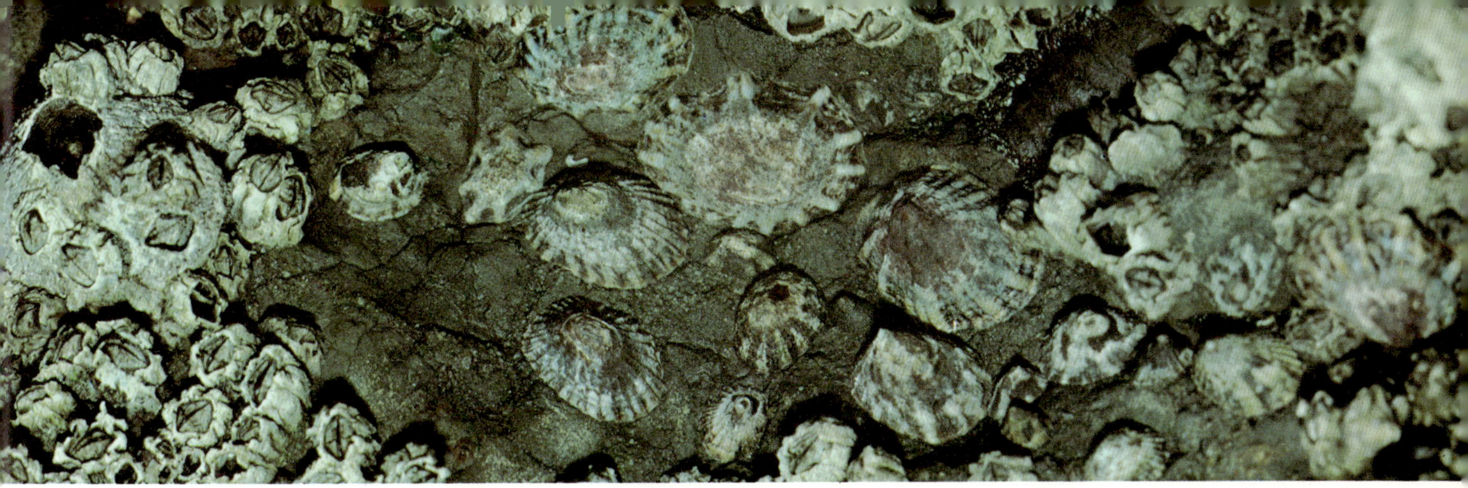

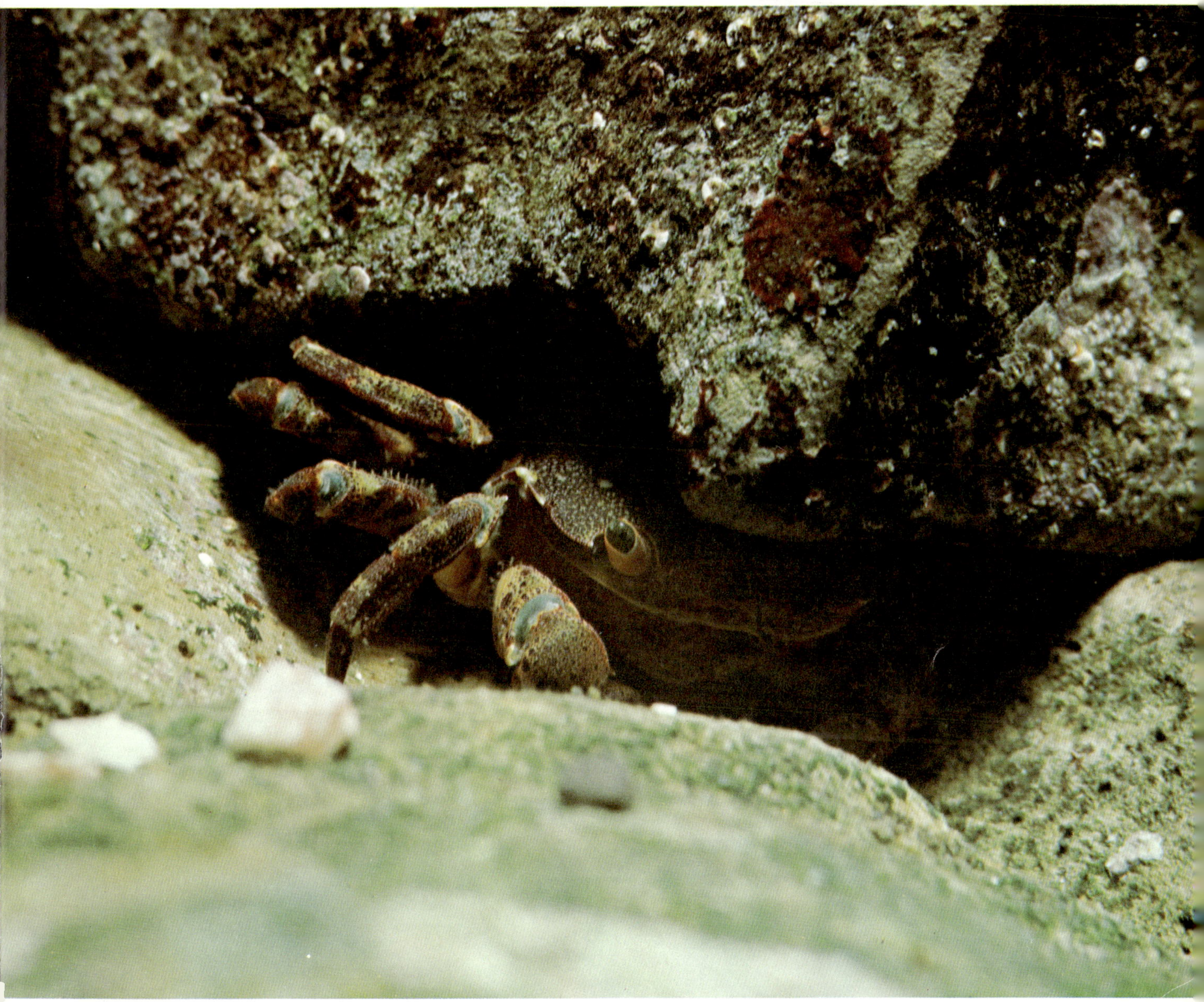

◀ **A shore crab feeds on a dead fish.**

This species of shore crab is usually active at night. During the day, shore crabs stay hidden under rocks on the beach unless they are tempted out of hiding by the smell of food.

▶ **A crab tearing its food apart.**

This crab uses its strong pincers to tear apart a dead fish.

Crabs are among the most common creatures of the seashore. There are many species, or kinds, of crabs—blue crabs, ghost crabs, fiddler crabs, and shore crabs. All crabs have ten legs and a short, squat body protected by a hard shell. But each species has adapted to seashore life in its own unique way. The back pair of legs may be especially designed for digging in the sand or for paddling in the water. The front pair of legs, often a set of large claws, or pincers, can be used for opening clam shells, catching small fish, or scraping algae from rocks. The crab also uses its pincers to protect itself from enemies, or predators, and to fight with other crabs. If a crab loses a leg in a fight, it has the remarkable ability to grow a new one.

● **A male and female crab.**

Crabs keep the back part of their bodies, the abdomen, turned under them. The female crab has a larger abdomen than the male. She uses it as a kind of cradle for carrying her eggs.

male   female

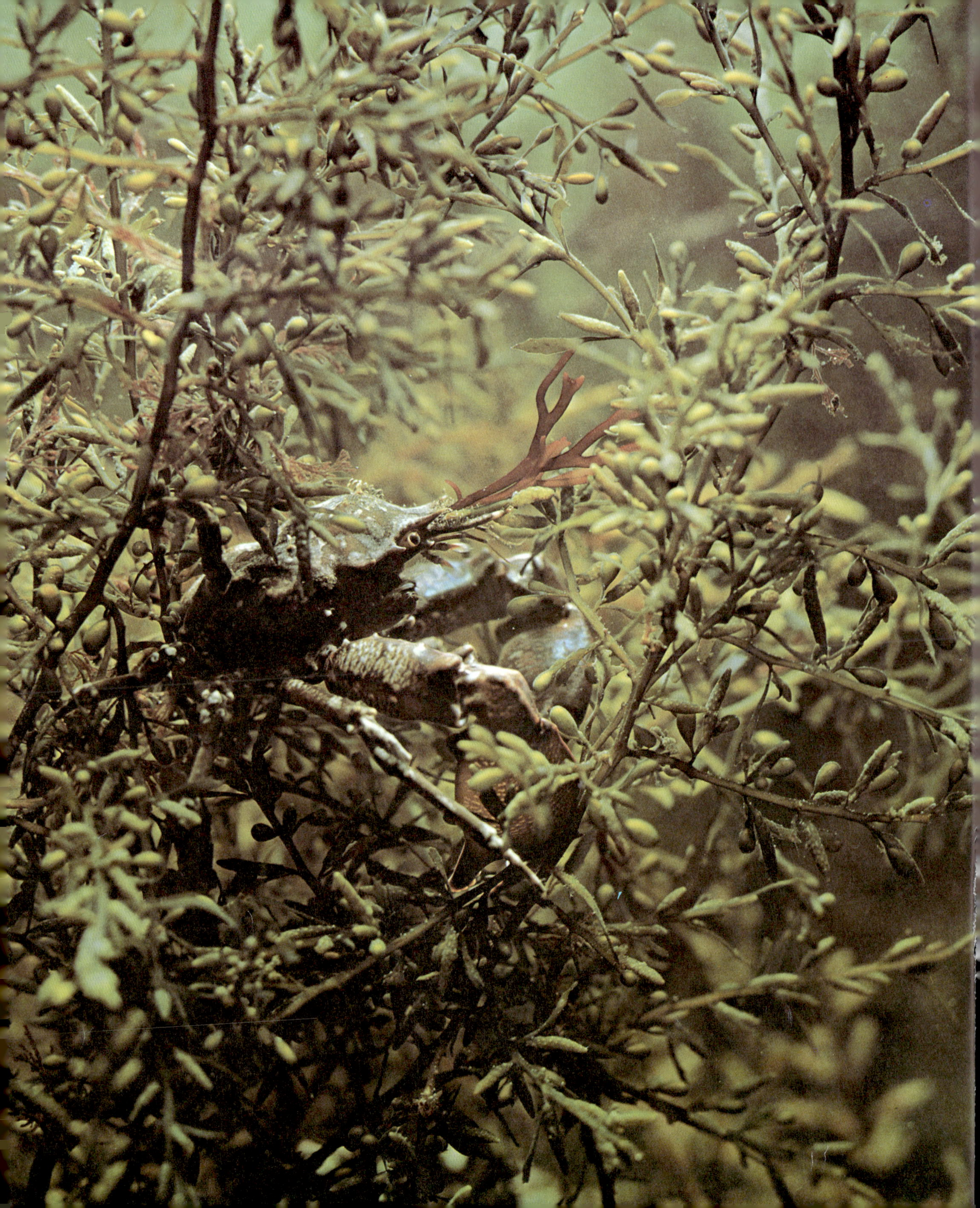

◀ **A crab hiding among seaweed.**

This species of Japanese crab cuts seaweed with its large claws and piles it on top of its spiny shell. When the crab moves to a new hiding place, it adds new seaweed.

▶ **A skeleton shrimp disguised as seaweed.**

Many seashore creatures are good at disguising themselves. This well-hidden skeleton shrimp belongs to the same family as shrimps and crabs.

Crabs are always in danger of being hunted, or preyed upon—by birds, fish, octopuses, and even by human beings. In order to protect themselves, crabs have developed ways of disguising, or camouflaging, themselves. Ghost crabs are so light in color that it is almost impossible to see them against a background of beach sand. Other crabs cut up pieces of seaweed or collect broken pieces of seashells and attach them to their shells so that they blend in with the beach environment.

● **Seaweed as shelter.**

Seaweed is a tough, rubbery plant that grows underwater. It has no roots, but it attaches itself to the surface of rocks. Seaweed offers shelter and camouflage for many sea animals.

A crab's spiny carapace, or shell.   A crab camouflaged with seaweed.

9

◀ **A tide pool.**

Pools of water that form in the crevices of rocks at the beach are called tide pools. Various kinds of sea animals live in them. If you add cold seawater to a tide pool, you may see animals begin to move around.

▶ **A green sea anemone spreading its tentacles (photos 1-4).**

This type of anemone has tiny green warts on its skin. Its tentacles are either white or purple.

Sea anemones are among the most beautiful and varied of all sea creatures. In fact, when anemones are feeding, they look like flowers, not like animals at all. Their long flowering tentacles, which look like flower petals, vary in color. They may be bright red, rich brown, dark green or orange. Others are striped or spotted in exotic patterns. When the anemone is not feeding, it pulls its tentacles inside its mouth. Then it looks like a small, round lump—not like its flowering self at all.

▼ **A closed anemone armored with bits of seashells.**

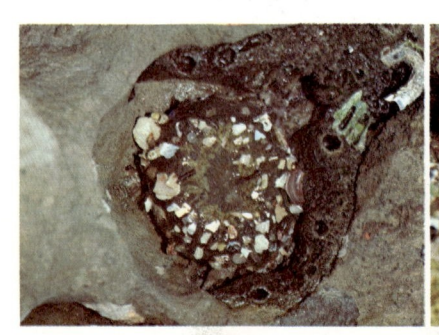

▼ **A closed green anemone.**

● **Closed anemones.**

If you find an anemone on a rock, it will likely have its tentacles pulled inside its mouth. If you touch it, the anemone will spew water from its mouth and make itself even smaller.

10

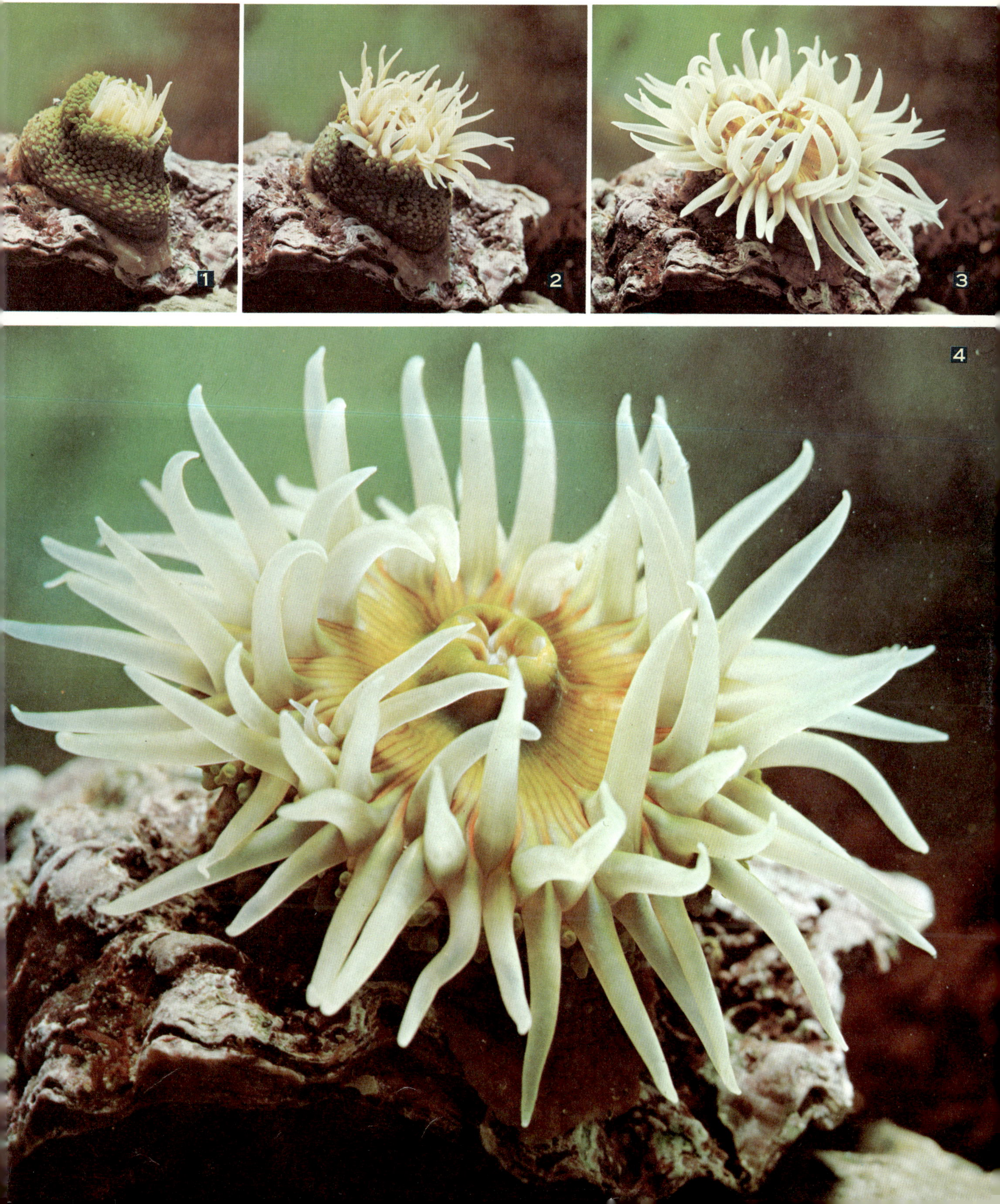
1
2
3
4

▼ **A sea anemone swallowing a fish.** Once it has stung a fish, the anemone holds it in its tentacles until it becomes weak. Then, gradually, it swallows its prey. Anemones have large stomachs and look like round bags after they have swallowed their food.

▶ **An immature anemone on seaweed.**

Some sea anemones split in two from top to bottom to form a new anemone. A Japanese species throws off tentacles one by one. Each tentacle becomes a new anemone.

The anemone is like a hollow tube with an opening, or mouth, at one end. When it ripples the muscles at the bottom of the tube, the anemone is able to move slowly through the water. As it bends its body, it extends its tentacles, searching for food. When one of the tentacles touches a small fish or other prey, it releases a small poison dart. The victim is paralyzed by the anemone's sting and is gradually drawn inside its mouth.

● **Some anemones anchor themselves.**

Some anemones attach themselves so firmly to rocks or shells that they cannot be easily removed. Others ride on the backs of crabs or on the shells carried by hermit crabs.

▼ An anemone swallowing a fish.

▼ A round anemone with its tentacles withdrawn.

13

▲ **A sea hare hiding behind rocks.**

Sea hares can often be found on the underside of rocks or among seaweed.

▲ **A sea hare crawling on a rock under water.**

This species of sea hare has two long feelers, or antennae, and many tentacles.

The seashells you find scattered along the beach once had living animals in them. Mollusks are soft sea creatures without backbones which usually live in shells. Oysters, scallops, clams, and mussels are all mollusks.

Sea hares are also mollusks. They belong to the snail family, but they do not have shells. Like snails, sea hares have a long flat foot for inching their way along rocky surfaces. There are many varieties and colors of sea hares.

◀ **A sea hare's foot.**

Like snails, sea hares have a long flat foot for crawling slowly about on rocky surfaces. The sea hare's mouth is located at the base of its antennae.

▶ A sea hare's eggs laid on seaweed.

▼ Varieties of sea hares.

(1) A Japanese sea hare, about three inches long. (2) A sea hare with gills on the sides of its body. (3) A Tsuzure sea hare. (4) A Kuroshitanishi sea hare. (5) A blue sea hare, about an inch and a half long. (6) An orange sea hare.

▲ A larch shellfish (left) and two white star-shaped shellfish.

▲ Sea snails on a rock.

◀ **A sea snail's foot viewed from underneath.**

Land and sea snails both have a large muscular foot. The foot is the largest part of the snail's body that can be seen outside the shell.

▶ **The top (right) and bottom (left) of a shellfish.**

This colorful umbrella-shaped shell belongs to the snail family. The mollusk's large foot, long antennae, and head are visible beneath the shell.

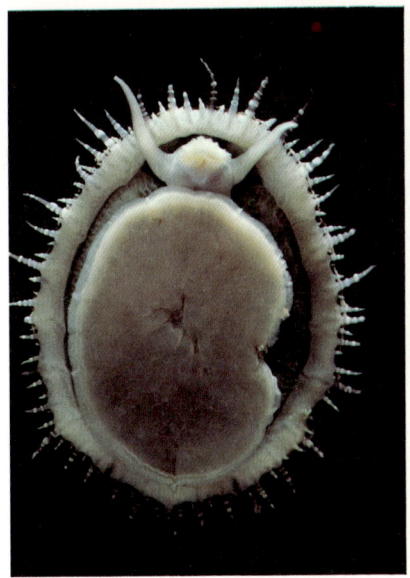

Although some mollusks, such as oysters and clams, have two hinged shells, snails have only one. The soft body parts of the snail are kept protected inside its shell. Sea snails, like land snails, have a large muscular foot that extends outside the shell. As the foot muscles contract, the snail moves slowly along, carrying its shell on its back.

Scientists believe that all snails lived in the water at one time because all snails have one thing in common—their bodies must be kept moist. Periwinkles are sea snails that no longer live underwater. Their bodies are kept moist by the damp sea air.

● **Periwinkles dislike water (photos 1-3).**

If you find periwinkles at the ocean and place them in a glass of water, they will eventually rise above the water. Although they are still called sea snails, periwinkles have adjusted to life out of water.

◀ **A shell of a large snake shellfish.**
This shell is about a half inch in diameter and is cemented to a rocky surface.

▼ **A large snake shellfish spreading a net.**
Like spiders, large snake shellfish make nets, or webs, in which they trap prey.

▲ **A fanworm's nest.**
This fanworm's tube-like nest is anchored to a rock.

▲ **A fanworm extending its tentacles.**
Fanworms spread their tentacles to search for food in the water. If they become frightened, they immediately draw in their tentacles.

The large snake shellfish cements its tube-like shell to a rock. Then it spews a sticky substance from its mouth and makes a net, like a giant spider's web, in the water. When its prey becomes trapped in the net, the shellfish pulls in the net and eats its victim.

Some types of sea worms, like the fanworm, build tubes, which they cement to rocks or seaweed. Fanworms spread their tentacles, as sea anemones do, in order to catch food.

● **Ornamental hairpin fanworms.**
This species of fanworm gets its name from its delicate feather-like tentacles (right). Many tiny fanworm tubes are cemented to this rock (left).

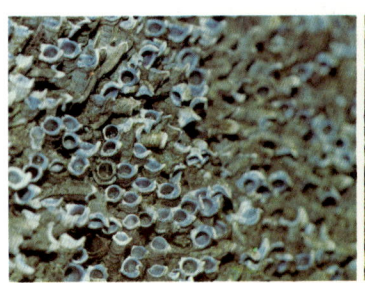

19

◀ **An infant rain sender.**
Rain senders live among seaweed. Several shells are embedded on their backs.

▶ **A rain sender swimming.**

▼ **A rain sender's shell.**

With its arched back and tentacles that look like ears, this funny-looking creature resembles a winged horse. It is called a rain sender, and it belongs to the sea hare family. But unlike sea hares, which don't have shells, rain senders usually have several of them buried on their backs.

When they are disturbed, rain senders discharge a purple or white substance that conceals them from enemies. It has been said that if a person bothers one of these unusual creatures, it will rain—because the shape of the liquid cloud it emits resembles that of a rain cloud.

Baby rain senders swim by fluttering a cloak-like film, or membrane, on their backs. But adults crawl, like snails, on the bottom of the sea.

◀ **A rain sender emitting a cloudy substance.**
When it is touched or disturbed, a rain sender discharges a purple or white substance. The substance is stored between the membranes on its back.

▲ **Various kinds of rain senders (photos 1-3).**

(1) An unnamed species of rain sender. (2) This type of rain sender grows as long as eight inches. (3) This kind of rain sender is often seen in the coastal waters of Japan.

◀ **Blue mussels on rocks.**

It is not easy to remove blue mussels from rocks because they anchor themselves with strong strings called byssuses. That is why they are not washed out to sea by strong waves.

The blue-black shells you see everywhere on the seashore are mussel shells. Mussels are mollusks. They are called bivalves because they have two shells hinged together. Mussels anchor themselves with strong threads to rocks so they will not be washed away by ocean waves.

Inside the shell, water passes over the gills of the soft-bodied mussel—as much as six glassfuls an hour! The gills sort out tiny food particles and also take oxygen from the water. Mussels feed on plankton, minute particles of plant and animal matter that float in the ocean.

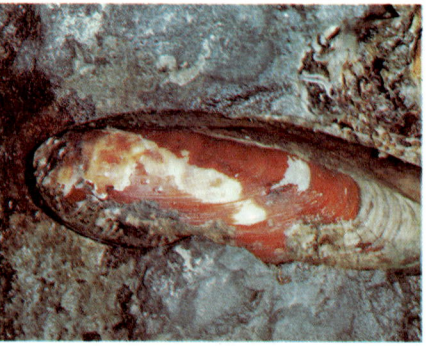

◀ **Bivalves living in rocks.**

Some bivalves use their shells to carve their way into rocks to make holes in which to live. The left photo shows a hole in a rock made by a shellfish. The right photo shows a shellfish which lives in a rock.

▶ **Rocks with many holes.**

If you find rocks with holes at the beach, you will know that bivalves have lived in them.

▼ **A shellfish living inside a rock.**

Bivalves live safely in rocks without being attacked by enemies. They take in seawater and plankton through tiny holes in their shells.

▲ Under the rocks at the bottom of the sea a number of unusual residents are hiding.

▲ **Unusual sea creatures.** (1) A flatworm, which crawls on the surface of rocks and eats shellfish meat. (2) A sea centipede. (3) An umbrella-shaped shell covered by the mantle, the part of the shellfish that makes the shell. (4) A group of sea squirts covering the surface of a rock. (5) A kind of shrimp. (6) Two crabs.

Beneath the rocks at the bottom of the sea, among broken shells and a tangle of seaweed, a host of unusual seashore creatures can be found. Among the most interesting is the sea urchin. The sea urchin is a ball-shaped creature covered with spines. Some tropical species have poisonous spines.

Tucked in among its many spines are tube-like feet with suckers at the end. The sea urchin makes its way slowly through the water, using its tube feet and strong teeth to pull itself along. As it moves, its teeth scrape off tiny particles of plant food from the surface of rocks.

◀ **Sea urchins on the underside of stones.**

These sea urchins have camouflaged themselves with seaweed. The thin white tubes are the shells of ornamental hairpin fanworms.

▼ **A sea urchin extending the tube feet among its spines.** The long extended tubes sticking out from among the spines are the sea urchin's tube feet. The hole in the middle of the spines is the sea urchin's mouth.

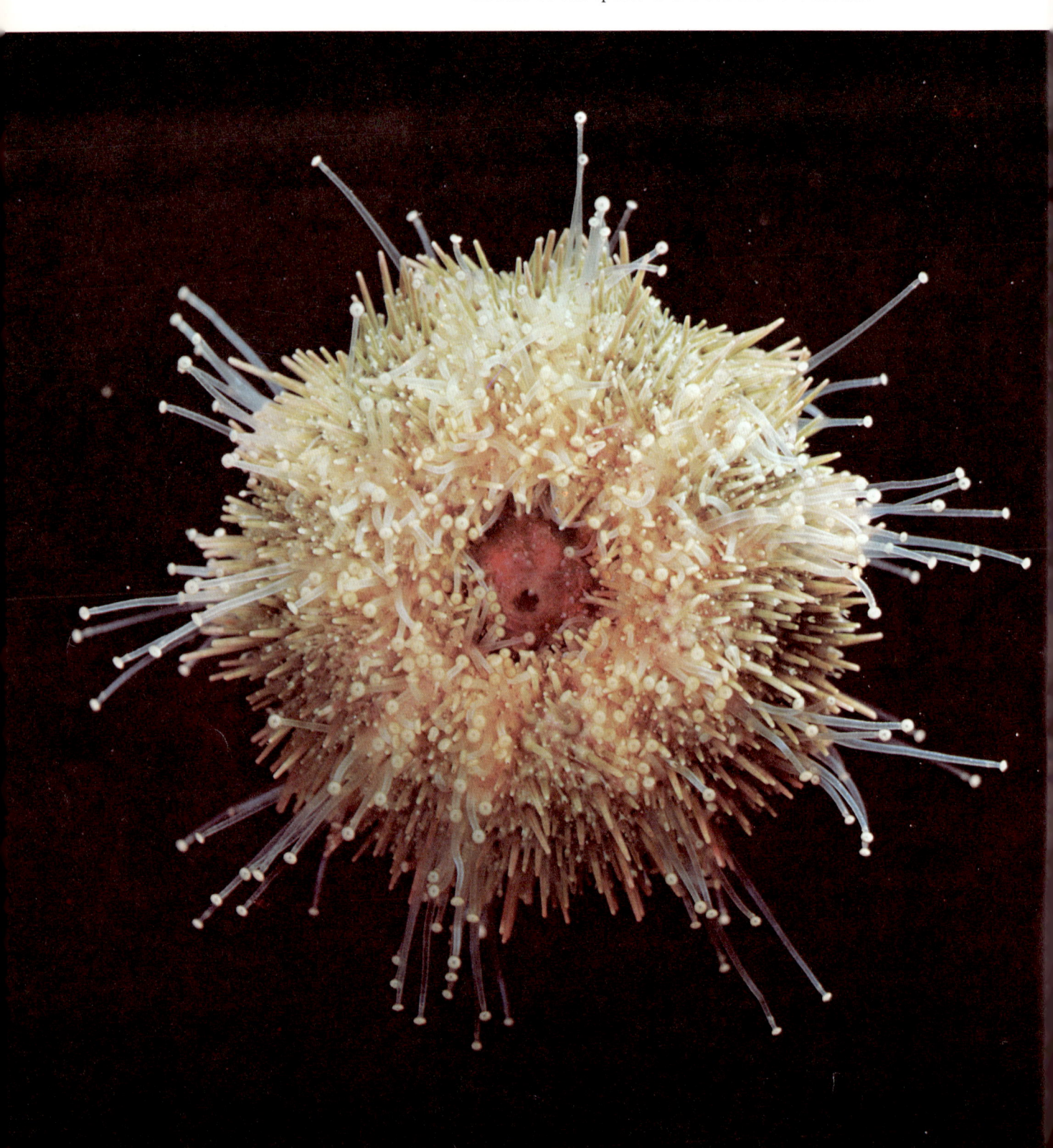

▲ A sea cucumber makes its way along a rock.

If a sea cucumber is touched or bothered by something, it discharges its internal body parts.

▲ A sea cucumber's body.

It is hard to tell one end of a sea cucumber's body from the other. In this photo, the left end is the mouth, and at the right end, water is discharged.

Sea urchins and sea cucumbers have quite different shapes. However, both animals belong to the same family, whose members have tube feet. And both sea urchins and sea cucumbers stay under rocks during the day and move around at night. Sea cucumbers expand and contract their bodies, the way caterpillars do, as they pull themselves along on their tube feet. Like sea urchins, sea cucumbers have symmetrical bodies—it is hard to tell one side from another because all sides look alike. But sea cucumbers do not have spiny skin, as sea urchins do.

▶ A sea cucumber's mouth.

Sea cucumbers use their tentacles to put sand and mud in their mouths, which they sift for small particles of food. Sea urchins have teeth with which they bite off seaweed.

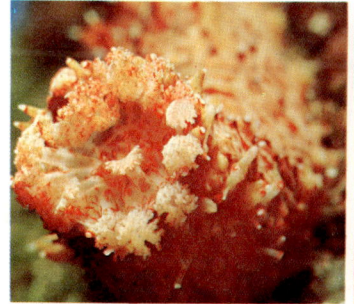

A sea cucumber's mouth and tentacles.

A sea urchin's teeth.

◀ **A starfish attacking a sea snail.**

The starfish uses its long arms to attack its prey. On the underside of the arms are hundreds of tiny sucking feet. In the center of them is the mouth.

▶ **A starfish eating its prey.**

When its prey is too big to fit into its mouth, the starfish turns its stomach out of its body. The soft, filmy stomach secretes a digestive fluid which breaks down the body parts of the prey, enabling the starfish to digest it.

Starfish are easy to recognize. Their long arms seem to form a star. But if you find one on the beach it probably will not be alive because starfish cannot live too long out of water.

Starfish are fierce hunters, or predators. They attack oysters, mussels, other shellfish, and even small fish. When it finds a shellfish, the starfish wraps its long arms around it and pulls until the shell opens up a crack. Then the starfish does a most unusual thing. It turns its big soft stomach out through its mouth and pushes it into the partially opened shell. When it has digested the shellfish's soft body, the starfish pulls its stomach out of the shell and back into its own body.

● **The starfish's arm.**

Starfish have no brains or eyes. But they have tentacles for touching and tasting and red spots on their arms which are sensitive to light. They have gills for breathing oxygen from the water.

A starfish's red spot and tentacles.

A starfish's gills.

▲ Various kinds of starfish (photos 1-4). (1) The pentagonal starfish has five points and is usually red or blue. (2) An eight-armed starfish. (3) The female princess starfish protects her eggs by holding them in her arms. (4) A spider starfish.

◀ **A hermit crab carrying a snail shell on its back.**

A hermit crab doesn't always carry its shell. But if it feels threatened, it runs quickly back to it. While true crabs step sideways, hermit crabs run backwards.

▶ **A hermit crab eating a fish.**

This hermit crab's long antennae stick far out of its shell as it eats a small fish.

While the bodies of most crabs are protected by a hard shell, the abdomen, or back part, of the hermit crab's body is exposed. So it "borrows" an empty snail shell to live in. As the hermit crab grows larger, it outgrows its adopted home and must search for a new shell. When it finds one, the crab uses its claws to measure the size of the new shell. Then it examines it, both inside and out. Finally, the hermit crab pulls its abdomen out of the old snail shell and quickly tucks it inside its new home.

▲ A hermit crab looking for a sea snail's shell.

▲ A hermit crab measuring a shell with its claws.

▲ A hermit crab backing into its new shell.

▲ A hermit crab carrying its new shell on its back.

GLOSSARY

algae—pondscum, seaweed, and other primitive forms of water vegetation. (p. 6)

bivalves—animals, such as clams or mussels, which have two hinged shells. (pp. 22, 23)

byssuses—strong threads or strings with which mussels anchor themselves to rocks. (p. 22)

camouflaged—hidden by blending with the environment. (pp. 4, 9)

carapace—a crab's shell. (p. 9)

mollusks—a group of soft-bodied animals without backbones, which usually live in shells, such as snails, oysters, clams. (pp. 14, 17, 22)

pincers—a lobster or crab's front pair of claws, used for catching prey and for protection. (p. 6)

plankton—tiny particles of plant and animal life that float in the water. (p. 22)

predators—animals that hunt and kill other animals for food. (p. 28)

prey—animals that are killed by predators. (pp. 9, 12, 18)

species—a group of animals which scientists have identified as having common traits. (pp. 6, 13, 21)